Jesus
gets Lost

© Copyright 1994 by Kevin Mayhew Ltd.

KEVIN MAYHEW LTD
Rattlesden Bury St Edmunds
Suffolk England
IP30 0SZ

OPENBOOK PUBLISHERS
205 Halifax Street
Adelaide
SA 5000
Australia

ISBN 0 86209 429 1

Printed in Great Britain

Jesus
gets Lost

Retold from Scripture by Rachel Hall
and illustrated by Arthur Baker

Kevin
Mayhew

Long ago, in a village called
Nazareth, there lived a happy
family: a father, a mother and their
son. The father's name was
Joseph. The mother was called
Mary. And the son – yes, you've
guessed – was Jesus. They lived in
peace with each other and with
their neighbours.

5

Joseph was the village carpenter. He made all the things the people in the village needed – feeding troughs for the animals, cots for the new babies, tables and benches for the houses, you think of it and Joseph made it!

And, of course, Jesus was always wanting to help Joseph. Like all children, he probably got in the way sometimes, but on the whole, he was a great help to Joseph. By the time he was twelve, he had learned all about making things.

Each year everyone in the village, and in all the villages around, went to the big city called Jerusalem.

They went for one of the most important Jewish feasts – the feast of the Passover. They all gathered there to thank God for helping them to escape from the wicked King of Egypt years and years before.

Some walked, others rode on donkeys or camels, and others went by cart, but go they all did!

The men went in the front of the procession, and the women went behind. The children could go where they liked, and, of course, it was great fun for them.

When the villagers reached
Jerusalem they went to the
Temple. Joseph, Mary and Jesus
went with them.

They loved the singing of the choir,
and the seven silver trumpets
which were always played on
important feasts. And they loved
the beautiful prayers thanking God
for looking after them. The
Passover was a very special time.

The villagers were not due to start for home again for a few hours, so Joseph, Mary and Jesus decided to look round the shops. They saw beautiful clothes, colourful mats, some very useful pots and pans and all sorts of delicious food. Of course, being simple village people, they were very impressed!

At last it was time for them all to go home again. Just as before the procession lined up – men in the front, women at the back. 'Jesus must be with Mary,' thought Joseph. 'Jesus must be with Joseph,' thought Mary.

Oh dear! Jesus was not with
either of them. What had
happened to him?

Of course, as soon as Mary and
Joseph found that Jesus was not
with either of them, they made
their way back to Jerusalem. They
were so worried about Jesus, and
they looked everywhere for him:
up one street and down another,
in the shops, behind walls, in fact,
everywhere a boy might hide.

But Jesus was not hiding . . .

19

Just as they were beginning to
give up hope of finding Jesus,
Mary and Joseph noticed crowds
making their way to the Temple.
'That's funny', they said to each
other, 'the Passover feast finished
long ago. Why are all these people
going back to the Temple?'

Never mind, – perhaps they would
find Jesus there. So Mary and
Joseph joined the crowd.

Well, Jesus was certainly there in the Temple. Not as one of the crowd though. He was with the Jewish teachers, called rabbis. What on earth was he doing there?

Well, believe it or not, he was
answering the rabbis' questions!
And the rabbis were astonished.
How could a boy of only twelve
know so much – about God
and about the way God wants
us to live?

We know the answer to that, don't
we: because Jesus is the Son of
God. But the rabbis and the crowd
who listened in amazement didn't!

At last Jesus finished talking to the rabbis and the crowd drifted away. Mary was very proud of all the things Jesus had said, but she was also rather cross. 'Why didn't you ask to stay behind in Jerusalem?' she said to Jesus. 'Didn't you realise how worried your father and I would be?'

Jesus answered his mother kindly: 'Why did you worry so much? You know I must do the work of my Father in heaven.'

But Mary and Joseph did not really understand what he was talking about.

Nevertheless, Jesus did as his parents said, and they all set off back to Nazareth. The other villagers were so glad to see Jesus safe among them again.

Soon everything was back to normal in the happy home of Nazareth.

Mary looked after the house and cooked lovely meals. Joseph spent his time in the workshop sawing and hammering. And Jesus loved and obeyed his parents. He learned something new every day. He was well liked by all the villagers, and he grew closer and closer to God his Father.

A note for parents:
This story can be found
in the Gospel according to Luke,
chapter 2, verses 41-52.